Opinions About
OCEAN
HEALTH

by Andy Sloan

TABLE OF CONTENTS

Ocean Health

The world's oceans cover 71 percent of the surface of Earth. They hold 98 percent of Earth's water. And they are home to 80 percent of the life-forms on Earth.

The oceans are a key part of Earth's environment. Life on Earth depends on having oxygen to breathe. Plants produce oxygen through **photosynthesis**. But oxygen is also produced by phytoplankton, which are tiny, plant-like organisms that live in the ocean. In fact, 50 percent of photosynthesis takes place on the ocean's surface.

Oceans also absorb and store carbon dioxide. This helps control the amount of carbon dioxide in the atmosphere. Too much carbon dioxide in the air is harmful.

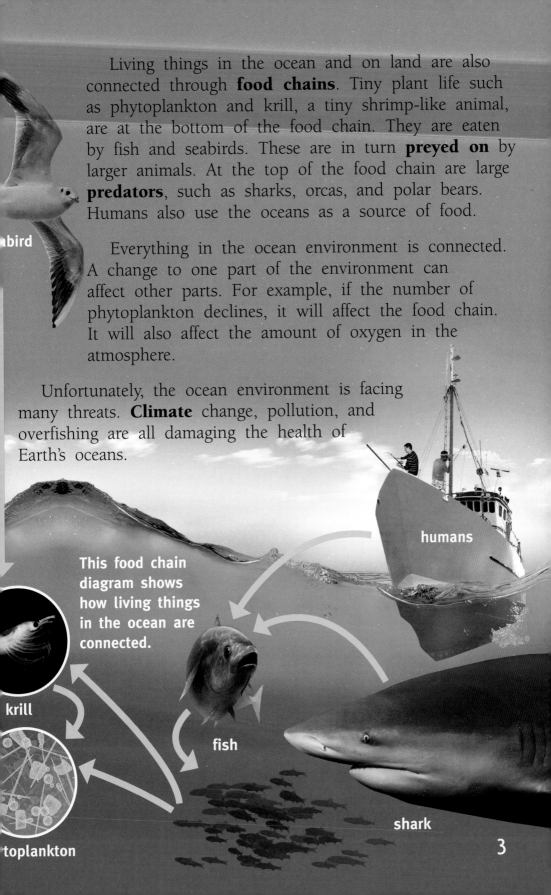

Living things in the ocean and on land are also connected through **food chains**. Tiny plant life such as phytoplankton and krill, a tiny shrimp-like animal, are at the bottom of the food chain. They are eaten by fish and seabirds. These are in turn **preyed on** by larger animals. At the top of the food chain are large **predators**, such as sharks, orcas, and polar bears. Humans also use the oceans as a source of food.

Everything in the ocean environment is connected. A change to one part of the environment can affect other parts. For example, if the number of phytoplankton declines, it will affect the food chain. It will also affect the amount of oxygen in the atmosphere.

Unfortunately, the ocean environment is facing many threats. **Climate** change, pollution, and overfishing are all damaging the health of Earth's oceans.

bird

humans

This food chain diagram shows how living things in the ocean are connected.

krill

fish

toplankton

shark

3

Climate Change

Many scientists believe that Earth's climate is changing. The world is getting hotter. Weather is becoming more extreme. Many scientists also believe that these changes are largely due to human activity.

Global warming is a part of climate change. Global warming is caused by an increase in greenhouse gases, such as carbon dioxide, in the atmosphere. These greenhouse gases are a natural part of Earth's atmosphere. They trap the sun's heat and keep the planet warm.

Power plants, factories, and cars all burn fossil fuels and release carbon dioxide into the atmosphere.

But when there is too much carbon dioxide in the atmosphere, too much heat is trapped. In the past 100 years, people have been using more and more coal, natural gas, and oil. Burning these fossil fuels releases carbon dioxide into the atmosphere. This has led to higher temperatures. Earth's climate has warmed about 1.4°C (2.5°F) in the past 100 years. Most of the change has happened in the past 20 years.

The Arctic Ocean provides one of the clearest signs of global warming. In the winter, the ocean is covered by thick sheets of ice. In the summer, some of the ice melts and breaks into pieces. But as the temperatures in the Arctic rise, more ice is melting every summer. Some scientists believe that by 2100 there might not be any ice during the summer months.

Arctic ice covers the least area each September. In 1979 it spanned almost 7.8 million square kilometers (3 million square miles). In 2011 it covered 5 million square kilometers (less than 2 million square miles).

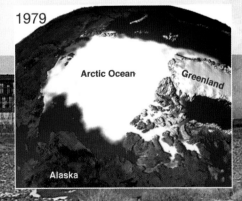

1979

Arctic Ocean

Greenland

Alaska

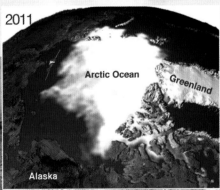

2011

Arctic Ocean

Greenland

Alaska

The shrinking ice has led to a loss of **habitat** for many animals. Polar bears live and hunt on the ice. During the winter months, polar bears travel long distances hunting seals. When the ice melts, polar bears have fewer places to hunt.

Krill usually thrive in the icy Arctic Ocean. These tiny animals are the main source of food for whales, seabirds, seals, and many types of fish. Melting ice and warmer ocean water make it harder for krill to survive. Scientists have seen a drop in the krill population in recent years.

Polar bears are at risk of losing their habitat.

The Arctic ice plays another important role in the planet's health. Land and ocean water both absorb heat from the sun. The Arctic ice reflects the sun's heat. This keeps the planet cooler.

When the ice melts, less of the sun's heat is reflected back into the atmosphere. Scientists at the National Snow and Ice Data Center explain that this creates a dangerous cycle. Warmer temperatures cause the ice to melt. When there is less ice, more of the sun's heat is absorbed by the oceans and the temperature rises. The ice will melt at faster and faster rates.

Warming temperatures can also cause problems in the other parts of the ocean. One study from Dalhousie University in Canada found that the population of phytoplankton has dropped by 40 percent since 1950. Warmer water in tropical oceans can kill coral reefs. This leads to a loss of habitat for all the living things that make their home there.

Krill feed on phytoplankton. In turn, many animals eat krill.

Pollution

Pollution in the ocean comes from many sources, including farms, factories, and people.

Many of the plastic products that people use end up in the ocean. The National Oceanic and Atmospheric Administration (NOAA) estimates that people put 635 million kilograms (1.4 billion pounds) of trash into the world's oceans each year.

Garbage harms sea life in many ways. Seals, seabirds, and other large animals can become trapped in plastic. Some creatures also accidently eat plastic, which can kill them.

This mound of plastic bottles (right) collected in a bay off New Caledonia, an island in the southwest Pacific Ocean.

The Great Pacific Garbage Patch is proof of the amount of trash in the ocean. It is a large area in the North Pacific Ocean where garbage collects. Most of the garbage is tiny pieces of plastic that float on the surface. The pieces collect in areas where the wind doesn't blow much and the waves are calm. Scientists estimate that two million pieces can be found in just one square mile of ocean. The pieces are so small that removing them does not seem possible. Scientists are researching how all this plastic can harm the environment.

Farming is another source of pollution. Farmers fertilize their crops and use pesticides to produce fruits and vegetables. Rain then washes these chemicals into streams and rivers. Eventually they flow into the oceans.

The fertilizers can cause algal blooms, which happen when there is too much algae in an area of water. The algae consume so much oxygen that no other living thing can survive. The result is a "dead zone" in the ocean. Today dead zones exist in the Gulf of Mexico and the Atlantic Ocean.

Factories and power plants can also spill dangerous chemicals into ocean water. Many of these chemicals, such as mercury, travel through the food chain. Smaller fish become contaminated with mercury. Bigger fish eat contaminated smaller fish and their mercury level builds up. For example, swordfish often have very high levels of mercury. They may be unsafe for humans to eat.

Oil spills are another source of pollution. Big rigs built in the ocean collect the oil from deep under the ocean or seafloor. In 2010 an explosion at the Deepwater Horizon oil rig in the Gulf of Mexico caused one of the worst oil spills in history.

The spill lasted three months. It affected life in the entire Gulf. Seabirds and turtles were coated with oil, making moving and breathing difficult. The oil harmed coral reefs. It seeped into the marshlands along the shore and killed both plants and animals. Shrimp, shellfish, and other fish became too dangerous to eat. Beaches and fishing grounds were closed. Hundreds of scientists from universities and environmental groups are studying the area. It will take years to find out what the full damage is.

Oil from the Deepwater Horizon rig gushed into the Gulf of Mexico for three months. Approximately 210 million barrels of oil poured into the water.

Overfishing

Cod, tuna, and many other types of fish have been an important part of people's diets for thousands of years. However, for the past fifty years, the populations of these species and other large fish have been dropping every year. More fish are being taken from the ocean than can be replaced by newborn fish. This is called overfishing.

Commercial fishermen have been finding better ways to fish since the 1950s. Many boats use large nets to scoop up hundreds of fish at a time. The nets can be as long as a football field. Others drag long lines—up to fifty miles long—hooked with bait. Sonar can help fishermen find schools of fish deep in the ocean. Spotter planes flying in front of the boats help fishermen search for fish in larger areas.

A commercial fishing boat crew might be able to catch 18 metric tons (20 tons) of fish in a day.

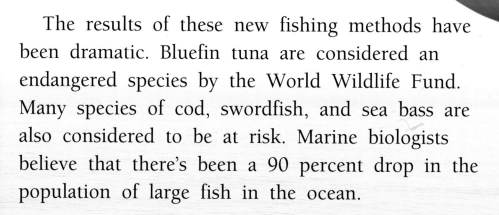

The boats also have large freezers to store the fish. This allows them to stay at sea for a long time and travel long distances to find fish.

The results of these new fishing methods have been dramatic. Bluefin tuna are considered an endangered species by the World Wildlife Fund. Many species of cod, swordfish, and sea bass are also considered to be at risk. Marine biologists believe that there's been a 90 percent drop in the population of large fish in the ocean.

It is not just the large fish that are in danger. Nets and long lines don't catch only the large fish. Sea turtles, smaller fish, and even seabirds can also be trapped. Fish caught in this way are called bycatch. Sometimes the smaller fish can be used by the fishermen. But most of the time the smaller fish are wasted. The World Wildlife Fund has reported that 27 million metric tons (almost 30 million tons) of bycatch are discarded each year.

People around the world depend on fish for food. The world's population is growing. In the 1980s, there were about five billion people on Earth. The World Bank estimates that today there are nearly seven billion. More people need more fish for food.

Many people in coastal areas also depend on fishing for jobs. When an area becomes overfished, thousands of people can lose their jobs.

The environmental group Greenpeace reports that "many marine ecologists think the biggest single threat to marine **ecosystems** today is overfishing." One possible solution is **aquaculture**.

In aquaculture, or fish farming, a body of water is the "farm." Fish eggs are the "seeds." Just as a traditional farmer decides what crop to grow and where to plant it, fish farmers decide which fish to raise and where. Fish eggs are first placed in a **hatchery**. When the fish hatch, they are brought to a bigger body of water. They are kept from swimming away.

Aquaculture causes problems of its own, though. Scientists from Greenpeace state that farmed fish can spread diseases to wild fish. Chemicals and waste from fish farms can harm the water. And farming fish takes away oxygen that other fish and aquatic life need.

14

Read and Evaluate
Opinions About the Health of the Oceans

You've just read about the role of the oceans in Earth's ecosystem. You also read about three of the greatest problems the oceans face.

Now read three writers' opinions about these issues. Each writer was given the same writing prompt, highlighted below. Each writer expresses a different opinion. But each opinion is well supported by evidence from the text. A well-written opinion piece states a clear position, has supporting reasons, and has a concluding statement. Skillful writers use linking words to connect their opinion to the supporting reasons. In the first opinion, annotations have been added to help you identify these important parts of an opinion piece. Which, if any, opinion do you agree with?

Opinion Writing Prompt

You have learned that the world's oceans are facing problems of pollution, climate change, and overfishing. In your opinion, which of these is the biggest problem facing the world's oceans? State a clear opinion and give supporting reasons based on evidence from the introduction and three sections.

Overfishing Is the Greatest Threat the Oceans Face

The writer includes a clearly stated opinion in the first paragraph.

Overfishing is the biggest threat to the world's oceans. If people continue to take too many fish from the ocean, many types of fish will become extinct. Billions of people around the world will have one less source of food.

The writer creates an organizational structure that lists reasons for the opinion.

The writer uses evidence from the text to support the first reason.

The world's population has grown very fast. There are almost seven billion people in the world, according to the World Bank. Many of them depend on fish as a food source. So far, fishermen have caught greater quantities of fish to keep up with the demand. But that can't continue. According to marine biologists, 90 percent of the large fish have disappeared from the ocean.

The writer uses linking words to connect opinions and reasons.

In addition, as the section on overfishing explained, some species of fish are becoming extinct. The World Wildlife Fund says that bluefin tuna are an endangered species. Other fish are also threatened. Once these species of fish are gone, they cannot be replaced.

Fish farming (aquaculture) can help increase the population of some fish, but it won't solve the problem. In fact, it brings its own problems. Further in the "Overfishing" section, Greenpeace notes that disease can spread from farm-raised fish to wild fish. Fish farming also causes pollution and can disrupt habitats. So we trade one problem for another problem.

We know that the world's population will continue to grow. We also know that fisherman will continue to take more and more fish from the ocean to meet the demand. If people do not address the issue of overfishing, there might not be any fish left in the ocean. That will be a problem for the whole world, not just the ocean.

The writer continues to use evidence from the text to support reasons and to use linking words to connect opinions and reasons.

The writer provides a concluding statement or section.

Climate Change Is the Biggest Problem for the Oceans

The world's oceans play many important roles in Earth's environment. The oceans are a source of oxygen. They also help keep the planet cool. Because changes in climate greatly impact these roles, it is the biggest problem facing the world's oceans.

Fish, animals, and people all need oxygen to live. Phytoplankton are an important source of that oxygen. However, research from Dalhousie University shows that the population of phytoplankton has dropped by 40 percent since 1950. Why? Warmer temperatures are killing the tiny plants. This will affect the amount of oxygen in the environment. And that hurts all things that breathe.

According to the section "Climate Change," Earth's climate has warmed by about 1.4°C (2.5°F) in the past 100 years. It says, "Most of the change has happened in the past 20 years."

Climate change also affects the ocean's ability to act as a natural thermostat. We know that Arctic ice reflects the sun's heat. This helps cool the planet. Scientists at the National Snow and Ice Data Center have proof that the ice is melting faster than ever because of global warming. This means that more heat is absorbed by the oceans. That makes temperatures go up.

Climate change causes many problems in the oceans. These changes will affect everything on the planet, including temperatures and the quality of the air we breathe. For these reasons, climate change is the biggest problem the oceans—and life on Earth—face.

Pollution Is the Oceans' Most Difficult Problem

Oceans are polluted by chemicals and fertilizers. Oceans are polluted by the plastics that people use every day. Oceans have been polluted by disasters, such as oil spills. Because there are so many sources of pollution, ocean pollution is the most difficult problem to solve.

Fertilizers used by farmers end up polluting the ocean. They slowly wash into the oceans from rivers and streams. As the "Pollution" section explains, this can lead to "dead zones." Even worse, poisonous chemicals such as mercury build up in fish that we eat!

Plastic is another source of ocean pollution. People use hundreds of plastic products every day. Then they throw them away. Unfortunately, many of these tiny pieces of plastic collect in the oceans. Scientists think that there may be almost two million pieces of plastic in just one square mile of the Pacific Ocean. If that is not bad enough, there is no way to remove these plastic pieces from the water.

Pollution can also come from accidents. The Deepwater Horizon explosion caused oil to spill into the Gulf of Mexico for three months. Scientists are still looking into the impact of this disaster.

Ocean pollution, and the problems it causes, must be stopped. To do this, people will need to reduce their use of plastics, chemicals, and fertilizers. People will need to think twice before drilling for oil in the ocean. Making all of these changes will be very difficult because people may have to make compromises in how they live. And that's why pollution is the biggest problem for the ocean.

Evaluate the Opinion Texts

Reread each opinion piece and evaluate it using the rubric below as a guide. Write your evaluation of each piece on a separate sheet of paper. Did the writers include the important elements?

OPINION WRITING RUBRIC				
Opinion Trait	**4**	**3**	**2**	**1**
The writer states a strong opinion, position, or point of view.				
The writer supplies well-organized reasons that support his or her opinion using facts, concrete examples, and supporting evidence from the text.				
The writer links opinions and reasons using words, phrases, and clauses.				
The writer provides a concluding statement or section that supports the position.				

4—exemplary; 3—accomplished; 2—developing; 1—beginning

GLOSSARY

aquaculture   (AH-kwuh-kul-cher) *noun* the farming of fish for food in a closed-in area (page 14)

climate   (KLY-mut) *noun* the typical or characteristic weather pattern for an area (page 3)

ecosystems   (EE-koh-sis-temz) *noun* communities of living and nonliving things interacting in one environment (page 14)

food chains   (FOOD CHANEZ) *noun* systems in which organisms use lower members of their group as food sources (page 3)

habitat   (HA-bih-tat) *noun* the place or type of place where a plant or animal naturally or normally lives and grows (page 6)

hatchery   (HA-chuh-ree) *noun* an area set up as a place for eggs to hatch (page 14)

photosynthesis   (foh-toh-SIN-theh-sis) *noun* the process through which plants use light energy to make fuel from carbon dioxide and water; also releases oxygen (page 2)

predators   (PREH-duh-terz) *noun* animals that live by killing and eating other animals (page 3)

preyed on   (PRADE AUN) *verb* hunted and killed by something for food (page 3)

23

Questions for Close Reading

Use facts and details from the text to support your answers to the following questions.

- Reread the first two paragraphs on page 3. Why is this information important for understanding the main idea of the book?

- What might happen to the whale population as a result of shrinking Arctic ice? Cite evidence from the text to support your conclusion.

- What specific information on page 10 suggests that mercury does not dissolve?

- What words on page 13 help you define *bycatch*?

Comprehension Strategy:
Main Idea and Supporting Details

Identify the three most important facts or details for each section. Then explain why they are important.

Section	Important Facts/ Details	Why the Facts/Details Are Important
Climate Change	1. 2. 3.	
Pollution	1. 2. 3.	
Overfishing	1. 2. 3.	